Oh

—

Cole Swensen

Apogee Press
Berkeley, California
2000

Deh! Non volerli vittime
(oh, do not let them be victims)
(Bellini)

to John Barnes

With much gratitude, I would like to thank the following journals in which some of these pieces first appeared:

American Letters & Commentary
Grand Street
Lingo
Ph
New American Writing
Yang

I would also like to thank Patti McCarthy and Beautiful Swimmer Press for publishing parts of the introduction and parts of 1 and 5 as a chapbook, and to express my warm appreciation to Keith Waldrop and to Jeffrey Burr for the enormous amount that each has taught me about operas, and to Lisa Wyant for enjoying them so much.

And special thanks to Eustachy Kossowski for the cover photo *A Panoramic Happening at the Edge of the Baltic Sea*, and to Stacy Doris for her help in procuring it.

Some phrases and lines that appear in italics within the body of text have been taken from the translations of libretti of various operas.

Book design by Philip Krayna Design, Berkeley.

ISBN 0-9669937-5-6. Library of Congress Catalog Card Number 00-134819.

Published by Apogee Press, Post Office Box 8177, Berkeley CA, 94707-8177.

Table of Contents

———

scale

the sheer face

smiled
in the half light

corps

the thousand

and the one

fit within

Oh

This matter of life or death on the tongue
        la langue

                  in every language it is

nom féminin
           what am   or did or done or ever have
      you gone
        the sea in its complexity/heredity/complicity
               rising
       all her
       anonymous
lung
resound
and resonant

tone:

                          the world would fit in your palm

               then

slip into your palm
something you wore at your throat on a chain

              belonged

written down

was from then on as written   as in sealed and carried
                                                    a letter to her sister

(take this letter to your sister)

                     (but this time it was real)

thus witness
this edgeless

she slits open

every instant   *Madame*

        holding the blindfolded
        by the hand

          while the other unfolds the single sheet

what shies
mine
either secret
    of the vein
        concealed for keeping   so very public

chorus of   cast as   down the

thousand warriors
        glint
        she hit the note
        and in the sunlit
all over
      was this utter

                    dissolved in speaking   further
                    unmoored by singing
          letter by letter
                                                  lay there lying
                         my
                         why
     with so much lithe and

                              flower.   An all-over
                                                slither the blade

                    cry for the maybe, the millions

    the Carmen

    when we were women

    throat unbuttoned

    by fire
                        by the fire
                        sewing,

reading,
raveling

        a slivered sun
              who

      ever married married you
             to
                 bit down / bite the tongue / stung

someone

at the door

as the woman falls
or is already fallen

thus
began once   and calls it home

and climbs the stair

and there called out
in a soft voice

"Mimi"
(now loudly)

opens the sea

like a floor   this flourish   this glint of the one

woman's drowning

surrounded

the rings on his fingers singing she cleft upon cleft
rent
open
open air   there   where there were
Lesson One:

any daughter of mine would die to sing perfectly

                                                            she sang

                                        O mio babbino caro

keeping time with the needle
in her hand
                        at her throat
                                        thrown open

There's a window on
                                the sea are

many things

slip by without name

———

What we today call opera began in the late Renaissance to recuperate a greatly berated and etc. They only wanted to recalcitrate the Greek chorus as a member of the household—a pet dog with a million legs, a servant simplified to a million names; you could call it now by name: Orfeo:

the world is your
          and will be this
                    dredged
                    this vertiginous harbor

opening how
we'd breathe for it,

                              would love to
                              breath in

                    its place   say grace
                                                 can be held

in a voice and left there

———

What we call today opera was born of a marriage between the mystery play with its edifying theme and the king as he came into the medieval city demanding singing, playing, dying and something that soaks up belief: Euridice:

                                        Breathe.   turned over
                                                                         in sleep to

                              look out the window

                              you see a million people

                    turns to salt

                                                    having forgotten the key
on the mantlepiece
having walked right out of the house

———

In Italian, opera simply means work and arose to address the Baroque thirst for extremes while the Camerata's concerns were simply that the words be both sung and heard. *Recitativo.* To be whistled on the way home. Night falling through the Florentine streets and Signora del Giocondo, now an antique, stops as she's sweeping out the bakery, thinking she's heard that tune before, or seen

it

or was it

                                    a smile or maybe a smell

but nonetheless recognized and there's some strange home

                        in a disembodied voice

                                    as proof

                                    against sight

                                    against flesh

                                    and that, yes

it's good to be known

———

so far beyond (said Rinuccini) all you
might say on the street and yet falling
so short of song he said this between
        novelty
                and harmony
                                in any case who
of a single voice   reigns alone
that rants alone while a crowd surrounds
that sings asides at the top of its lungs
        (I ever am) it says it sang
Ah me! Ah me! What dawn brought down
to its setting   *the sun of my eyes*
remain secret
             in
             violet
       I sing (= I sever)   I scream
(= I never have and will never

Peri, Jacopo (1561-1633) ordered:
"grievous tritones for the tale of Euridice's death"
"grievous tritones for Orfeo's heart erased" grief
as all else, breaks down to three

that will stop and wake up

that a touch disrupts   and/or

                                        must divides

                    Ah me

E vero
(It's real)   (This is real life)
(This is a photograph of real life)
(This is the only chance you'll have at real life)

ONE: Leaping

Enter a celebrated diva who enters the Chapel Sant'Andrea della Valle and mistakes the voice of Angelotti for that of an unknown rival as her lover paints the Magdalena as the fleeing revolutionary exits as the flames of Rome (later to become sheer sound) (you find yourself humming the tune) as Scarpia walks in, occasioning an unsavory but not untimely little piece of irony based on inversion and entrance and dies (once more on time) as the war dissolves and the painter is fired and Floria Tosca takes her gracious leap into previously unoccupied space.

See Floria fly

         See, that's what it means to fly
See, that's what they promised you
all over

        and longer   grace

is disappearance

          turns to sky

made to be seen from a distance

            insist on it

and its interlocking parts   entire crowds

                                                                    strokes

on some

and the landscape grows

beyond a personal sorrow

                    a breeding marrow

takes face

                    and if my voice

                                        fail me
                                        some greater society

                    flames

               in flames:

               somewhere a child smiles

      strangely

Scarpia

folds at the waist

         "I'm dying and I remember you"

         (blue

pooled)

         that life beyond life that greater

         city state

    so the voice subsumed

so ignites

                              (someone in the audience coughs)

and the passport rests half written

where a *we* is inserted
implicated
                    presumed

to say yes
                 kill him for us

                                        folds at the waist

in crowds

During one performance in New York, the stage hands were so affronted by the prima donna's prima donna attitude that they placed, instead of a mattress, a trampoline below the parapet just before the leap and thus see Tosca rise again, twice, thrice

                    she holds the knife in her hand
throughout the introduction, the intermission
and takes it home

———

"I thought I heard

(was paid to hear)

       that everything lives
that lives
       under the tongue

       are the burning stones

       that the room grows
huge
       while on stage each
single part of a mechanical clock

and the fleeing man moving
so slowly out of the dark

———

and flayed the tongue against a thousand of them
flung out   entire   in form   in which
                                      watch

      what becomes

        (arranged)

ornate   at the top
                           of the lungs

Oh God such humiliation such pain

        (I sing therefore I sense
some descending   oh god so much
        annihilated
           to
"her heart in her mouth"
(and her mouth hanging open like that)

---

where the throat deforms to
                        sound
                        resounding
in its single link
from height to ground
that opens   mouth to mouth

and wide of it
that simple
sky on a hinge

Letters

In several cases a letter is delivered that changes everything; sometimes we see it being written but never can we see (key though it is) the letter itself and yet, in this form in which the voice is all, unfold the darkened voice to roiling ink which errant ailes far from the body, that only, which can be entire she: she is and will; having said seals, having sent lives on, which is to say a life of its own is this betrayed.

but her brother got there first
with a paper knife

tremble in the weight

pale

keeps opening

sudden as a sheet

applied it to the dark

"Oh how I am foolish"

and had it hand-delivered.

                                        A woman at her window
                                        A woman at her wedding
and one waiting
                                                signed just above the date
                        unto seal
and to signet:
whatever bears is

Please forgive

my haste

she left   behind on the table
                    she meant it for
                    and was undone
Replica.
          Incredula.
                              Rare as spice
                                             and thrust it from her
                    folded voice.
                    A voice
turned back on itself and slipped
unto sent. And what did you mean and if it is
and, in some way, a way of holding

                              between   or simply
          hover there   we live   on air

—
37

TWO: Knives

Enter center stage a gypsy woman and a Japanese maiden who find that they have certain points in common with an itinerant player whose husband can't get his make-up on straight so the robins must return alone high up in the mountains where the thinner air makes the cards more clear and the play must go on as the crowd roars and the bull goes down and "the people are paying and want to laugh here" and the fact that it happens on stage doesn't mean it isn't really happening.

Some are willed self
To some it is a deft
swift and
            knew exactly what
doing as she did

"anything sung is always in the present tense"

some would not give in

Putain
                in which we heard

every word

                conceals a name, annealed, came
over the sea
arranged her escape
put on his make-up crying

        One fine day we'll see

(le corna)
I shall
hurled into flight
don't ever find out
like arrows
cleanse
lightning
outspread
      rain
         Un bel di vedremo

with the arm drawn back at the elbow

Otello

but only after

a long time after

                    (and have no regret
                      after you've grown up)

a woman making cigarettes
slips out for a bit of sun

                  streams on
                      and thrown
(la fleur que tu m'avais jetée etc. cherry
blossoms, *traditore*, and everywhere
it's Spring.

and the cards give the other women
exactly what they want

        they give   just
                       want
                       what did   you and

why did you come
                  some
thing hidden perhaps stored
under your tongue
          like a stone
          like they bury with the dead
          to hurry them on

behooved
          unscored

(The body turning (back) to word.)

(You who came to me from Paradise)

(You whom some heaven has handed on)
(she says to the child)
You who've fallen through entire skies
(Note: here: again the vehicle is air:
You have fallen to me through years and years of air.

———

dressed
in a thin dress
        said
              no matter

              what and no

and so the story fades
        leaves only its effects: broken things:
                    breath
                    (wealth)
                    what stays
gold   and later   glint
among the (what was it that you
              (and yet can be reduced to

(refused to or got used to
(or to distill)

       and the moment that arched, that spread and then branched
       out and these things that won't and utterly
                         and then she
                         said
and then said again
    and rewrote
                the message   out loud
emerged
    a living
        singularity
                  (thus)
          takes up   (therefore)
there's no more room.

(once I had these

        of all of them

          things)

         and walks on

and from now on

at home built
sheet of it upon sheet of light
          (there's a tooth that curls in bone)

that screams on key
that streams on through   strung   knows
        its course   a woman knits in a window
                everything to dust.

THREE: Fires

Enter a Druid priestess and her lover and his lover while there are other worlds—pearl and woman, yearn and "I

am reading the arcane volumes of the sky." Don't find out. "Je crois entendre encore." And therefore, will love again, which falls on him who has just mailed away his heart. Wore his necklace inside out. Means I saved your life. Once (I think I still can hear) this went up in flames, a shaped blaze, little blades rising.

                    Of multiple
and militant order

                                   that light is power

that matters
that we remember

                         that love quite simply
turns body to lantern

                                        (Chorus: *Guerra, guerra!*)
              or rather
              as you so wish it, leave
but alone
                                        (Chorus:
        Sangue, sangue!)
                         have this to give
twice life to the child
and to the other child
                         life a second time

                    by which
we   (one for each)
cleansed   they say
flame cleans

the hallways of the bones
the ventricula of vows
the sliver   *who silvers*

                                        these sacred ancient trees
(translated stone and wood cell by cell to sound)

turned life
by stages into heat and   *let not*
one escape

                              but to

                    sooner heart to sooner this
                                        ever
                              in the presence of

red and

lung and fusion

       built and arched the rib

                           it all immured

and remained. Maimed

           cathedral of trees

              an elemental claim on the nature of

return

                     has been

and she

sealed.   What din   in the trees. What steel leaves.

———

We lay back on the beach
cleanly, shining, slightly

                                        incarnate sieve

are there repeated
            slightly
chilled in the breeze off the sea,
lightly warmed in the sun
(This is what it's like inside the sun.)

Noir:

a woman walks down a street with time on her hands—

                                        paganism

                        allows the face to multiply

                        and with it the voice which is yet

                        is always headed back to singularity. The insistent
                        dimension of intention, of choice,
of all that, which has all   (been done before, Love (said as a
                                        proper name, as someone
you knew and now know
                        (turning at the window

the letter into glass
the

what you had
in your hand

that lived
around your neck
increasingly intricate
you'll walk out

and the world
will have exceeded itself

a little
entire
it always involves
a slip
(something always slips)

———

Carry under your tongue, the human body in molar state.

An therefore inhumanely ornate

       went out

dressed to kill   and watched

       who dies   once (upon a time)

                  I:

To marginate, to
put the self off to the side, to move outward in an imperceptible
slide (from the body, evenly

                  necessary: crowd scene

(once they were

                thousands, once we were

                      choked the streets
barely   contained
factories

of you could leave

                    opposed to law
        what strident flinch

                          learns *no* first

            and dust and dirt

                    (unto half my kingdom)
and will not fall.

FOUR: Gasping

Here the dominant decor is respiratory problems loom large. There are women for whom it just doesn't work out. The catalyst in the slow cases is simple circumstance: it's so easy to be born in the wrong place, to fall in love with a broken man who breaks. Violetta, Mimi, Desdemona. A letter, a muff, a scarf, enter a plea for "good" women, enter winter inexorably wedged between lovers enter anger and insist on its veracious eye when each in the house finds a woman entering a box, a fistful of white flowers in her fist enters dying stronger than a living woman enters in love against. It's in the air; you see it coming down like snow or at least like something white that presses close, a virgin's dress, a slip of cloth that did not belong to someone else.

to those who die of breath
or the lack of it
to you are given

                                    with your enormous

all exhaling
colors and the colored

                        breath coiled
(feel it fill your lower back
just beneath the ribs)
Grips.
Shifts.

                        They're all innocent.

Elaborate. —

            "You crawl toward something all your life."

She saw something slip past the window so she went to the door.
(This part of the story is true.)
Breathe in.
Breathe deep.
Open the window; I can hardly

But irony

(what really happened)
        The endless exercises.   (she's lost her key)
Scales.   (camellias in the hall)
                and the taste of air
                            (a simple square of cloth)

doth.
both.
quote.
            all.

and out the window she saw

                                        rising in her own lung

          water of fire
          white shape coming down

The handkerchief in his pocket was her own.
key gone and candle cold
                                        This is how

The carriage pulling away down the drive
The small fog on the pane from her breath

                  you watch it moving out

You say that's what you meant.

It's slow.

      It's snowing outside in Paris it's Christmas
      It's snowing outside

You love the white, too, just the fact that it's white.

There is one red dot

                        there in the white field

           now two now ten

           so many

                years spent learning to breathe in just right

                        in the middle

he dropped a torn petal
rubbing it in

                        You've been
and no one else will enter the room.

While in Desdemona's case
it happened all at once;
fifteen years of tuberculosis
in the time it takes to sneeze.
It's like snow.

            Your breath stands out in the winter air.
Clear.
All there.
Count it now.

Desdemona turned and stared
                       for a few hundred years
             from a long way off
there's a ghost
                    dressed in breath
      that slowly gains
legs and arms and eyes
designed for someone else.

———

Thought and action
cancel out in a glaze at the skin

in the brand of the face

God help me to hide the anguish in my heart

I have just this minute come from the boat

(reduce to turning points)

"You must leave"
"Do not go"

(that swell to fill)

until they touch

"*Leave me*"
"*I love you*"

took almost nine years to write

there is nothing but

Tchaikovsky fell in love
with Tatyana   and so said yes
to Antonia

"*Farewell forever*"
"*You are mine*"

By the time he writes

"oh my

                    different

"oh

                    be whispered

("after death she was so

FIVE: Glances

Enter a look that could kill and then does and from whence and there Eurydice falls (it's her job) while the lack of one for whom a glance would save, Salome gravely watched from just beyond the stage the world ends in a stepfather begs and you will have his head as he will have her voice: ghost that clicks through the lungs of the house with a violin that means some-thing else and you have sold us to an ugly one, my most vituperative tongue. And the head arrives and she dies of it. And he can't bear her cries and she dies of it. And then she dies.

In the word *glance*, you hear glass

                                                         just once

                        every

love
louvers a gap   a pit   a part of him
remained intact

                         was law
the ever arbitrary

                            girder
                            wording
                            line
                                           as in
                     one strives and as
              one falls

don't look
it's not nice

                  Someone in the audience coughs

      He fell in love at first sight

from the back of a mirror

there really is a lake down there

is a bottomless pit

cries to have never been

        seen
        "If you

had seen me you would have loved me"

and dies with the lights on

If   *love's mystery is greater than the mystery of death*

        "I have kissed your mouth"

I have heard the oath
felt the tooth
tasted salt you thought you were alone

It takes
all our eyes upon

                              to even start
          and turned around
          and loosed the word
          and worked the lights
          so that in that light
          the white face sliced
who

could have saved

                    in a glance

that became

                              "It becomes you, my dear, it

changed.

—
70

(chorus: the body)

becomes

Have seen me,
thus
and
then
this
         which so exalt the surface: a world
of immanence, of eyes
with their brace of dimensions   no matter how curved they lie   I
believe. It will open out forever with nothing underneath.

COLE SWENSEN's previous books include *Try*, winner of the Iowa Poetry Prize and the San Francisco State Poetry Center Book Award, and published by the University of Iowa Press in 1999, and *Noon*, winner of Sun & Moon's New American Poetry Award and published by that press in 1997. *Numen*, published by Burning Deck Press in 1995, was a finalist for the Pen West Award in Poetry, and another earlier book, *New Math*, was selected in the National Poetry Series in 1987.

She also translates contemporary French poetry, fiction and art criticism, and has received grants from the French National Bureau du Livre and from Fondation Beaumarchais as well as residencies at the Camargo Foundation and the Atelier Cosmopolite at Royaumont.